W9-BJK-129

Animals on the Farm

by Teddy Borth

ABDO
ON THE FARM
Kids

Visit us at www.abdopublishing.com

Published by Abdo Kids, a division of ABDO, PO Box 398166, Minneapolis, Minnesota 55439.

Copyright © 2015 by Abdo Consulting Group, Inc. International copyrights reserved in all countries.
No part of this book may be reproduced in any form without written permission from the publisher.

Printed in the United States of America, North Mankato, Minnesota.

032014

092014

 PRINTED ON RECYCLED PAPER

Photo Credits: Shutterstock, Thinkstock

Production Contributors: Teddy Borth, Jennie Forsberg, Grace Hansen

Design Contributors: Dorothy Toth, Laura Rask

Library of Congress Control Number: 2013952559

Cataloging-in-Publication Data

Borth, Teddy.

 Animals on the farm / Teddy Borth.

   p. cm. -- (On the farm)

ISBN 978-1-62970-050-2 (lib. bdg.)

Includes bibliographical references and index.

1. Livestock--Juvenile literature.   I. Title.

636--dc23

2013952559

Table of Contents

Animals on the Farm

Many different animals live on the farm. Cows, chickens, and sheep can be found on a farm.

4

Animals make things for the farm. We get milk, clothes, and food from farm animals.

Cows

Cows make milk that people drink. That milk is also used to make cheese, butter, and ice cream.

9

Goats

Goats also make milk.
Goat hair can be used
to make clothes.

10

Sheep

Sheep grow hair called **wool**.
It is made into warm clothing
and **blankets**.

12

Chickens

A female chicken is called a hen. She lays eggs that people can eat.

Pigs

Pigs are very smart. Pigs have a great **memory**. They can remember where food is kept and how much is left.

16

Dogs

Dogs are good workers. Dogs have a great sense of smell. A dog uses its nose to find animals and plants.

18

19

Horses

Horses help around the
farm. Horses can pull
heavy **equipment**.

More Facts

- Farm animals are known as "livestock."

- Goats can live in places cows cannot, such as mountainous areas.

- Sheep are among the first animals to be kept by humans.

- Pigs have a great sense of smell like dogs. Pigs are used to find **valuable** mushrooms.

Glossary

blanket - a large covering woven from fabric. It is used to keep a person warm.

equipment – supplies that are necessary for a service or action.

memory - to remember what has happened or what has been learned.

valuable - something worth a lot of money.

wool – the soft, curly hair that grows on sheep and other animals.

23

Index

abdokids.com

Use this code to log on to abdokids.com and access crafts, games, videos and more!

Abdo Kids Code:
OAK0502